WOW FROM LOVE TO YOU

Designed by Heather Curtis / hcurtisdesign

ISBN 978–1–0690698–0–1
Printed in China by BookPrintingChina

WOW

FROM LOVE TO YOU

MARTIN MAHEUX

CONTENTS

INTRODUCTION

IN THIS WORLD WE LIVE IN, I FOUND A WAY TO BALANCE LIFE AND MAKE IT WOW EVERYDAY. This discovery happened unexpectedly, without me knowing what I was looking for.

In fact, this book was written utilizing a continuous flow of WOW energy.

This is the energy that allows the human body to work at its absolute highest level. This includes our original human pristine powers. I did not initially know about these powers. They came to me through a series of synchronicities. I then intuitively explored these powers for myself.

You cannot fully access your pristine powers until you bring your light energy to the highest level.

When I am writing about the highest light energy, I'm referring to the WOW energy vibration one finds within and which remains activated as long as one can stay in the present moment.

Last year, I partially experienced this WOW state with a girlfriend. However, every time her fear programming would kick-in, she would leave the now moment, which eventually led her away from me and out of the relationship. This stressful situation happened just two months before I had to move my cafe to a new location. I was heartbroken and running on minimal light energy. Yet, a month earlier, I began applying the principles found in this book more deeply (maybe my intuition was preparing me for what was around the corner!).

I thought to myself, perhaps that peak of love energy I had experienced with my girlfriend could be extended to my daily light energy. I decided to hold loving thoughts for her and invited that light energy into the stressful moments of re-locating my cafe.

What were the results? I created an amazing new cafe in 12 days when others thought it would take two to three months to get all the permits and various trades to do the work and complete the renovation! My intuition led the way and I found myself proceeding with zero fears.

All coordination happened in WOW energy. Everyone who was needed to complete the project showed up in perfect timing.

For example, on the second day I realized I needed someone with a pickup truck to remove old materials from the demolition. Five minutes later, a friend, Steve, showed up and asked if there was anything he could do. The synchronicity here is that he is the only friend I have with a pickup truck and he has no cell phone for me to contact him.

The whole project flowed perfectly and no one involved understood what was happening, including myself.

On opening day I sat in my cafe, exhausted but so happy. Unbelievably, the cafe was filled to capacity with customers, jazz music playing in the background. I sat there wondering: "What just happened?"

Even though I was heartbroken about my lost relationship, I managed to thrive on high love energy by creating it within myself and projecting it outwards. WOW, what a ride!

I'm so grateful for the experience of high love energy I had reached with my ex-girlfriend. It was something that I had never experienced before. I am now able to trust that I can accomplish anything, keeping love flowing in my life.

Staying in love frequency is what kept me connected to the WOW energy.

It became clear to me that I was transforming into a different man: one with different powers. These are powers humans have always had but due to our programming as we grow up, we lose the ability to use them.

I began a search online to see if I could find others with similar experiences. I investigated scientific and spiritual sources hoping to find relatable information but nothing profound stood out or really satisfied me. My experience was quite different. This book will explain my findings.

For some readers, this book might feel weird as it may be too far from their personal beliefs and conditioning. When I think of myself reading this book six years ago, I would likely not have completed reading it because only now do I know that I was not ready for this information.

Writing this book was not entirely my idea. A friend of mine, Lawrence, a retired editor, came to my cafe one morning and said, "Martin, you know what we should do this winter? Write a book!"

I looked at him very surprised and in that same moment wondered what exactly could I write about? After about 10 seconds of reflection, I said "It takes time and energy to write a book."

Lawrence replied, "It was only an idea. We've had very good conversations about life and happiness. Your life perceptions and how you are always happy and able to remain there, it's all very unusual and worth writing about. Think about it Martin."

I answered, "I will, Lawrence. Thanks for putting that amount of faith in me."

My interaction with Lawrence was an important synchronistic event. It stayed in my mind all day. That night, I was doing a meditation and clearly saw the cover of a book, a blue cover. The calling to write a book was slowly happening.

The next day, I was parked in my camper van looking out over the ocean and decided to write down some ideas. I grabbed one of my notebooks, placed it on my legs and started reflecting on whether I had the time to do this project. I wondered if I knew enough about how to write a book? And why would I even want to write a book anyway? I looked down at the notebook that I had placed on my lap and saw the word "Blue" at the bottom of the back cover. This sign sealed the deal. That's it! I'm writing a book and the cover will be blue.

After a week, I met with Lawrence again. We agreed that I would start writing and see how the process unfolded. When I returned home that day, I sat down to write but couldn't find the first words.

I went to bed and woke up at three a.m., thinking very deeply about the book and the side conversation I had with Lawrence the day before. We were talking about his house and his uncertainty about renovating or moving. I suggested that he see himself as "being the house" and feel it energetically. My belief is that we are all made of energy and can flow with everything around us. This thought now inspired me to "be the book" and WOW, so many ideas suddenly began to flow.

I AM THE BOOK

LET'S DIVE RIGHT INTO WHAT CAME THROUGH.

I have always wanted to help people have more ease, flow and joy in their life, so it was natural that my energy would flow that way.

This book is about the "machine", the most amazing machine ever built and so unique that no two are alike. The machine I'm referring to is me, you and every other human in this world.

Let's go back in time for a moment. For the past 25 years, I have been hearing the limiting belief, "I'm not good enough". Like many of us, I used to believe that I was not good enough and was always looking for ways to be better. Better at everything. Better than others. But how could I be content in this situation?
Let's see how?

Our machine is so amazing, yet we don't even know how it works. Our machine didn't come with an instruction manual.

Let's think about us as souls in our machines and now we are going to learn how best to use it.

Start by looking at your machine. See yourself standing at a close distance where you have a view of your machine.

» What do you see?
» What do you feel looking at your machine?
» Would you like to change something?
» What would you like to change?
» How healthy is your machine?
» Is your machine up to your standards?
» Looking at it, do you see a joyful or anxious machine?

I guess, like me when I did this exercise for the first time, you are probably thinking that you would like to change something or for sure that you don't have the best machine ever.

Learning to use your machine properly will create a higher intake of light energy and will bring it to a new potential.

You will be able to use your machine in the way it was originally designed. This may seem very complex but my theory is that you are the reflection of your machine. This is why I first want you to understand how your machine works.

Once you do that, everything will flow and you will have clear access to the collective consciousness. Your life purpose will then come to you through intuition and synchronicity. You will be able to take your machine anywhere you want in harmony with the flow of life.

Many of you who have read books on self-help, motivation, consciousness, mindfulness, etc. know that those books are helpful but from my point of view, I would start with addressing the machine and then the powers that have been forgotten over thousands of years will arise. Very few had or have access to those powers but they are there ready to be used.

The faster you understand the importance of bringing your machine back to its ultimate functionality, the faster your soul will thrive within it. Your soul and your machine have to vibrate on the same frequency for the true WOW to happen and be felt, and to automatically reactivate all your human pristine powers. Some may ask what is that frequency. The frequency that I found that works best is the one that comes from love, surrender and trust.

Your soul is part of the Consciousness-of-All. It has all the information that ever existed and it will be available to you when you are able to use your super powers.

On the first breath you took, your soul came into your machine. It connected your machine instantly to everything by its vibrant energy and will stay with your machine to your last breath.

Imagine the three parts of your brain: the left side, the right side and the frontal lobe. The frontal lobe has access to the past and future.

Now, imagine a big chair in your frontal lobe. See yourself sitting in it and look around. On the left, you see a big wire that is plugged into the wall, the inside of your forehead. The wire has complete access to your past. Stand up and put your two hands on the wire and unplug it. Nothing will be erased. You will take a break from your past stories, limiting beliefs and traumas.

Now, on the right you see another wire that is plugged into the wall. That's the future that is always trying to direct you in ways that your conditioning has been telling it to. You are going to do the same as before. Unplug the wire for now. You already unplugged the past and now you are unplugging the future. This brings you to the present.

Now, your machine is waiting for instruction.

The information you need is already evolving in front of you without you noticing; it is the present at its best working for you. Don't worry about anything in your past or future.

Your light energy can only rise in the present.

LIGHT ENERGY

LYMPHATIC

WHAT DO I MEAN BY LIGHT ENERGY AND ITS OPPOSITE, DARK ENERGY?

First, it is important to realize that everything is energy. It is within us and around us, and in everything we do.

It can fluctuate at any time.

We can be influenced by light and dark energies without knowing it if we are not aware. It is important to be able to identify those energies in our environment.

There is a spectrum of energy. To better understand its effect on us, I have arbitrarily chosen a range from -1,000 to +1,000 units of energy a day.

The calculation of your daily energy will help you to visualize where you lose or gain energy. Through this process, by increasing your light energy daily, you will eventually be able to use the powers that have been dormant in you.

I have purposely left out most references to dark energy because I don't want your energy to flow there. Thus, I focus primarily on light energy. Where your attention goes, your energy flows.

Energy Calculation

The following chart contains examples of my experiences with energy levels. You can use these levels as a starting point. After you gain a deeper understanding and awareness of what creates light and dark energy, you can make it more personal for yourself.

This list is based on how much light energy you can gain or lose in a day.

Walking	60/hour
Walking in nature	80/hour
Running	80/hour
Running in nature	120/hour
Mountain biking	130/hour
Alpine skiing or snowboarding	130/hour
Paddle boarding	130/hour
Yoga	150/hour
Meditation	200/hour
Working at a job you like	50/hour
Indifference at a job	10/hour
Disliking your job	-50/hour

Breathing techniques	30/10 minutes
One glass of water	20
One glass of structured or distilled water	40
One glass of milk	-20
Raw fruit	30/portion
Raw veggies	20/portion
Handful of seed or nuts	50
First cup of coffee or black tea	30, additional cups -20/cup
Herbal tea	30/cup
A meal of raw fruit and vegetables	150
A meal with animal products	-150
A meal of processed food	-150
Drinking alcohol	-100/glass
Smoking marijuana	-100/joint
Being with a good friend or family member	200
Being in love	500 to 1,000/day
Being in a healthy relationship	200/day
When a relationship breaks up	-500 to -1,000/day
Living in the past	-200/day
Worrying about the future	-200/day
Worrying about money	-500/day
Being anxious	-300/day
Being happy	300/day
Doing creative things you like	200/day
Giving time to someone	200/day

THE SEVEN PRINCIPLES OF LIGHT ENERGY

WE WILL NOW LOOK AT HOW THE SEVEN PRINCIPLES WILL HELP YOU CREATE LIGHT ENERGY FOR YOUR MACHINE.

Principle One: Air

Energy is in the air everywhere.

When you are breathing, your soul is moving inside your machine.

Your aura is a reflection of your soul vibrating outside of your machine.

Light and dark energy is in the air everywhere.

Let's imagine that you can see a spectrum of colours coming out of other machines. All those colours are around them at all times. When you are getting close to other machines, there's the possibility that you breathe in those colours (parts of their energy). The colours have little particles that could contaminate or help you depending on the amount of time you spend in their presence.

Sound travels in air through vibrations. All the air and sound on the planet is the aura of Mother Earth.

In nature you can hear birds singing, the waves of the ocean and the wind in the trees. Mother Nature always emanates beautiful music when she's happy.

Is it the same with your machine? It will create beautiful music when it is happy. It will chant, sing or whistle.

Since I raised my light energy to high levels, sometimes I start singing automatically when I am happy.

I encourage you to research various breathing techniques and find some that resonate with you and then practice them regularly.

For example, starting with five minutes of a breathing technique a day could add 30 energy units. With practice you could increase to 15 minutes for 90 energy units. You will find your own ideal level for the best functioning of your machine.

That's the first principle of the machine. Before doing anything else, be conscious of where you are breathing and how.

Principle Two: Fuel

The machine needs fuel for functioning. The question is, what is the ideal fuel and how much?

This could be a very sensitive topic for some readers. There are many different fuels you can use depending on how you want to live your life and how much you want to awaken your super powers. The right fuel will do it. It is the most powerful principle for that.

I propose, based on my own experience and my research, that the ideal fuel is organic plant-based whole food, as much as you feel like and as much raw as possible.

Have I lost some of my readers? I told you this was going to be sensitive. Before giving up, please stay open-minded and keep nourishing your machine with what you think is best for now until you finish reading this book. Afterwards, you can experiment with my proposed fuel and see the results for yourself.

If you have been putting any other fuel in your machine, some type of cleanse might be good to consider once a month for a period of time, or as needed.

In my light energy chart, fruits, vegetables, seeds and nuts are light energy. They range from 10 to 50 per serving. If you eat them on a daily basis, they will light up your machine. Every system in your machine will start functioning together at a higher level.

Why is that? These foods are full of light energy from the four elements: the rays of the sun, from the air, from water and from the soil.

The rain, air and sun bring information to the ground, the ground to the tree and the tree to the apple for us to eat. We are on the continuing line of light energy from the sun to us. The four elements help create the best fuel for your machine.

These foods also bring information from the Consciousness-of-All to your machine, which you want for your evolving consciousness. The Earth contains so much information for us to gather and assimilate.

Until I was 44, I ate a lot of animal products, starches and processed-food. From when I was 19 until I was 44, I worked first as a chef and then I owned three restaurants at different times. I know very well the love of that kind of food and the lifestyle that comes with it. Now that my fuel is plant based, I have new energy and powers. This is greater than anything I have ever experienced. It is the first time that I have felt that I have an in-tune machine.

I'm sharing what I believe and what has worked for me and many others. My choices are for the ultimate functioning of the machine.

The best way to start that I can recommend is that you switch your present diet, whatever it is, to 50% raw, 50% organic and 50% plant-based food.

Mother Nature will see your willingness to change and help her. She will, in return, provide all the information that you need to progress in your health and the awakening of your super powers.

If you think 50% is too easy, go to 60%, 70% or even 100%. At 100%, you will vibrate at a high frequency!

Principle Three: Water

Imagine walking in the desert for days without water and you see an oasis. You're running towards it and you start drinking the water until you are satisfied. Imagine the love you have for the water at this precious moment, the body-water connection, the importance of the water and the respect you should have for it at any time in your life.

I believe that water has memory and carries information to you from nature.

There are ways to energize water. For example, being grateful for every glass of water and expressing positive affirmations, such as "This is going to be the best day ever", will automatically transform your water into a higher light energy level.

The more love you put into your water, the more light energy you get.

Principle Four: Play

Your machine needs movement that is playful. Walking, biking, yoga, running, hiking, dancing, swimming and any other playful activities will harmonize your machine at the ultimate level.

The more you enjoy the movement that you are doing, the more beneficial it is. Always have something planned to move your machine.

Look at all the energy units you gain with movement as shown in the light energy chart.

The more you move, the more energy you get.

Principle Five: Rest

Rest is vital for your machine to function at high light energy.

Lots of machines do not rest or sleep properly. As soon as you bring your light energy to a higher level, your sleeping and resting will be so much easier and more restorative.

When sleeping, if your machine is full of light energy from the other principles, that will help your machine to repair, rest and be ready for the next day.

The rest principle will always depend on the other principles and their energy.

Also, in the machine, we have 11 organ systems that must function nicely for it to rest or sleep efficiently. When one organ system doesn't work at its best, the others try to help.

For example, if the nervous system is overwhelmed, it takes energy from the other systems and that will prevent the machine from functioning the way it should and simultaneously create a machine that cannot rest properly.

A happy machine with high light energy will always have good rest.

Principle Six: Nature

When you enter a natural environment, like a forest, lake or ocean, you are entering its energy field, its aura. The intelligence of nature

scans you and automatically feeds you with light energy that it knows you need.
We are from and part of Nature, which has been classically described as consisting of earth, air, fire and water. The machine is from and thrives on these four elements. You can recharge your machine by interacting with these elements, such as sitting under the sun, swimming in a lake and walking barefoot.

Plants have helpful information for you. Let Nature know that you understand that.

Connect with nature on a daily basis. You will be surprised what messages or information will come to you.

When you are in nature, ask questions, say thank you, and sing. That will help Nature to help you.

Nature created you and will inform you of everything you need to know through light energy in the present time. It's the flow of nature, the flow of life.

Say "Hi" to Mother Nature every day.

Principle Seven: Relationships

I am very excited to write about this principle.

While on Earth, you are going to have experiences with others. Since your machine is made of energy, you will automatically be reacting to the energy of other machines.

I'm going to explain my view about light energy in a love relationship first. This is where you can gain the most energy in a day but, more importantly, it is critical to understand that some relationships can deplete you of most or all of your light energy in the same day.

For friendships and community, it is pretty much the same as for a love relationship, except the impact on gaining or losing light energy is less.

You need to add up the energy from the other principles to understand this one. The total of all the other principles represents the love you have for your machine.

A Love Relationship
If you are in light energy from the first six principles and fall in love, your light energy can reach or even exceed 1,000 energy units a day.

However, at the start of a new relationship, a nice person may have a tendency to give away too much light energy from their first six principles which they would normally use for themselves. In order to have a healthy loving relationship, it is very important to feel a true exchange of energy.

Below is a scenario that explains how light energy is affected in a relationship.

Julia has very good light energy from the first six principles with an average of 400 per day and starts a relationship with Logan at an average of -200. These energy levels reflect their love for their machines.

Julia is a very happy and energetic person. Now by falling in love, she goes over the maximum of 1,000. WOW, she is in love. However, since she expends lots of energy on Logan (500) by being very attentive to him and the relationship, her light energy is now between 700 to 1,000 depending on the day.

Logan's energy rises from -200, where he was not really caring for his machine, to an average of 600 from falling in love with Julia, which gives him a good feeling of what love energy is. Since he expends 200 on the relationship with Julia, he is now at 400.

Julia's light energy now ranges from 700 to 1,000 and Logan is around 400. WOW! Everything appears to be running smoothly, even though there is a difference in energy levels.

Julia and Logan's relationship brought lots of new love energy into their lives. They are helping each other with their addition of love energy.

Logan's positive energy of 400 is because of the relationship. The problem with this situation is that love energy can evaporate very quickly when something goes wrong, which could put him back into dark energy in an instant. Let's say after a time, Logan loses 400 because of his conditioning and his recurring negative thoughts.

Julia feels the love energy evaporating too. She is now losing 500 because she has doubts about the relationship and sees Logan dealing with dark energy most days.

She goes down to an average of 200 per day. For Logan it's even worse, he goes down to zero.

If there is poor communication between them, each one will begin to imagine or think about what might have happened. Doubts, anxieties, jealousy and more will create dark energy on both sides.

Let's minus Logan and Julia another 500 as their relationship has deteriorated, putting Logan at -500 and Julia at -300.

It is difficult to love someone when you don't have enough love for yourself.

Some days are better for them but where they are now is not suitable for a loving relationship.

Logan can't get himself together and most of the time he doesn't get energy from the relationship with Julia. He feels depleted and is having thoughts of having to get energy somewhere else. Most of his thoughts and solutions are not good for this relationship.

Julia is feeling depleted as well. She isn't used to being in dark energy and this kind of yo-yo situation. She will try to break up with Logan. However, she feels very weak because she is missing the high energy from love and she is not as strong now as she was before meeting Logan. This is why she will try everything to save the relationship, even to the point of losing all her energy.

Weeks go by with many short break-ups initiated by Logan, until finally he decides to break-up permanently. Until he does the work on his first six principles, he will always need the energy of others to help him be happy in life and succeed in a loving relationship.

For Julia, it is hard because now with the breakup, she's having negative thoughts about what went wrong, why he couldn't love her, and why everything she does can't bring him back. She is now down to -600. She's missing the high love energy and all the future dreams that she created with him. Until she completely closes the door on the idea of the relationship with him, she will continue to lose light energy.

I was in the same situation as Logan in my early life. I was mostly in dark energy.

I have used the first six principles to bring myself into positive light energy and appreciate who I am, making it easier to be alone or with someone.

Caring for yourself first will help you. It will also attract and inspire others to be at your level of light energy.

When you are in a positive light energy, your intuitive power is reliable. Listen to it. If you feel dark energy in some situations around someone, it's because it's there and you should not doubt yourself.

Pay attention to your energy level. If you go under half of your light energy, recognize that this is the first red flag. Take one step back before going down any further in energy and breathe (principle 1). Go for a walk in nature (principles 4 and 6), perhaps with a friend (principle 7) and rest as needed (principle 5). The principles are there to bring you back to self love.

The power of love is so big that it can cause you to give up all of your light energy to get it. That's a gamble. Be careful!

It is the same thing when a breakup happens. You could drop 1,000 instantly.

When that happens and you lose too much energy, you must let go of everything about that person. Where your attention goes, your energy flows.

Rebuild yourself quickly with the principles. Keep unplugging the past and future that you built with that person as often as you need.

When you bring yourself back into the light energy, all the powers of your machine will start functioning to help you. Don't worry if some days you fall back. Keep your attention on the seven principles. Don't forget love energy is also in Nature and all around you.

When you are receiving light energy from someone that transforms into love energy, don't take it for granted. Be grateful to have it. Take the time to enjoy love in the present moment.

The same applies to community, family and friends. Surround yourself with healthy energizing people and practice elevating energy with them. Make sure you are getting or creating light energy simply by being with them.

When a friend has good light energy for you, this will make a smooth and loving energy exchange. The words that your friend uses will be beautiful, and you will feel relaxed and safe around that person.

Be aware of your energy shifting. If you are in light energy, your intuition should be correct. If your vibrations change around that person, it's the first warning sign to be aware of. Communicate this with them if you are comfortable with it. That can help a lot for raising both energies.

When you have finished a conversation with someone, ask yourself, was that an intake of light or dark energy? It can be easy to discern. Ask yourself, did I receive or lose energy? If you don't know or cannot feel it, call it neutral.

By talking from love, you have a possibility to change any energy exchange. Inside everyone is light energy but for some it's hidden behind conditioning, fear and trauma.

To not deplete others and yourself of energy, always take three to five seconds before responding if you think your words will hurt or create dark energy for others. Stay silent and offer only your presence. A shift in the other person's energy needs to happen first to bring light energy to the table but until that space opens, keep your light energy.

Never underestimate the force of light energy. Only use it with love and respect for the level of energy where others are at.

The relationship principle, more than any other principle, is about understanding the power of love.

Applying The Principles Of Light Energy

When should you start applying the seven principles? Now!

A simple way to get started is to be grateful for your beautiful machine, the best ever built, so unique to you.

You are probably thinking, "How long will it take to feel changes?" You can feel it in as little as one to three weeks. How much benefit you experience will depend on your commitment, discipline, intensity and actions.

I understand that my readers are at different places and levels of energy at this moment in their lives. It might be difficult for some to act on all the principles. This could be because of their present environment, such as their job, family, fuel, beliefs or stories. No matter what, I suggest you start without thinking too much because past conditioning or future anticipation will prevent you from taking action.

Just go for it: surrender, love and trust.

The Consciousness-of-All and Mother Nature will recognize your willingness to start being part of the high light energy experience and will help you.

THE ENERGY OF CONDITIONING

DIGESTIVE

EARLIER IN THE BOOK, I ASKED YOU TO UNPLUG THE PAST AND FUTURE. Your machine is then in the present.

Should you keep it unplugged for good? Yes. You will not need it.

When your machine runs on high light energy, everything will be in the present. You will understand with greater clarity that many of your worries were attached to your conditioning. These worries will go each time you unplug yourself.

In a relationship, don't follow your conditioning on who you think you should be with, what they should look like or how successful they are. If you use your conditioning to make this decision, it will cause you to think of the future. Focus on the energy that emanates from the moment. This will lead you to a consistent intake of 500 to 1,000 light energy units a day.

Your conditioning can stop this flow from happening if the nervous system is overwhelmed, preventing you from focusing on the present.

Anything that does not match your past conditioning or best experiences from different relationships will make you worry, and you might not take the chance on a potential partner. Trusting your present self is the way to go.

A healthy machine will let you know if your potential partner feels like WOW or not. That's the energy that I'm talking about; it's an energy that is always effective in the present moment.

You need a healthy working machine first, then everything will start to connect with your intuition, which will eventually bring you the power of trust within.

Rather than projecting on a partner what you think they should be, simply be with them for a coffee, for an hour or for the day. If being together brings you energetic intake and time feels like it stops, that's the beginning of creating love energy and you will know it.

Get out of your machine and look at it. What do you see? Do you see a WOW machine? You should see love energy between the two of you. That's what you want. Trying to feel the WOW by looking in the past or in the future will distract you from the WOW in the present.

Also, some people create a lifetime of future projections of what a relationship should look like from their conditioning. They will discover, usually later, that they were living from their conditioned ideas and have never really lived a relationship with love emanating from the present.

Now let's explore the conditioning of the feelings of joy and happiness. If you follow your past conditioning or future expectations, you may experience a false sense of WOW energy and be trapped later in something that doesn't feel good. You have to get the WOW feeling in the present.

For example, I will be happy when I own my house or when I go on vacation.

Doing that creates expectations for the future from your conditioning which can create unhappiness in the present. Simply being in the present should create joy, regardless of the situation.

It's possible to feel joy at work just by being in the moment and being grateful for it! For example, don't think of why you don't like your job or some of your co-workers. Instead, be grateful for the ones that you like working with, saying their names out loud when driving to work. Be grateful for all the people that you will be interacting with today. Give thanks for having a job for this moment, even if it's not the ideal job yet. That will create joy within.

Some common situations in life that affect our conditioning are schooling, marriage, family, savings, owning a house and religion.

If your reality is about following your conditioning, then that's what you will be doing for most of your life. The other option is to restart your machine, stay in the present and follow your intuition, and synchronicity will guide you. The ride is amazing!

My conditioning started 50 years ago when I was born. I believe I also had previous conditioning in my genes from my parents.

If I keep my 50 years of conditioning, while trying to manifest the next 30 years of my life, it will feel like my present is equal to 80 years moving back and forth in my head, telling me what I should be doing with my life in the present.

My proposal is that you focus on one day. When you wake up, you should be ready for a new intake of energy and not be controlled by thoughts about the past or future.

Anything from your past that you have accumulated as conditioning may contain inaccuracies for the moment you are living now. The truth you need is accessible in the Consciousness-of-All, in Nature and in the present when you have a healthy machine. You have to surrender, love and trust.

I'm asking you to let go of any conditioning for now, even the idea that this book is new conditioning. See this book as a new idea or synchronicity in your life. By the time you finish reading it, new truths will be available in the present for you.

MANIFESTATION ENERGY

URINARY

I LEARNED ABOUT MANIFESTATION FROM A BOOK WHEN I WAS 19. The message was that you could manifest anything you want.

I followed the instructions and my first success that I remember was manifesting my dream car. I put a picture of a new Mercedes 500SL convertible on my fridge in 1992. It was my dream car at the age of 19. Eleven years later, I was driving to my restaurant and saw that exact car for sale at a car dealership and I stopped to ask about it. The sales person told me the details and I traded my car right away. After an hour of paperwork and bank arrangements, I drove away in my dream car. At that moment, I thought Wow! I succeeded! I made my manifestation happen. I couldn't believe I was driving my dream car.

It took three days for me to realize this car was not really my ideal car at this phase of my life. It made me feel amazing for a few days, was beautiful to look at and very fast but there was no space for my mountain bike or anywhere to seat more than one passenger. It also used a lot of gas.

Without really knowing, over the years, I manifested girlfriends, businesses and money. However, none of my manifestations felt right long term and the feeling of WOW soon evaporated.

My mom always said, "You got what you asked for."

Some people make a vision board to manifest their future. Do I recommend you do this? No. From my perspective, this limits the flow of your life.

Don't get me wrong! Manifestation is a real thing. I believe in the ability and powers that humans have to manifest but I do not recommend it.

For example, if you want to manifest a big house in a very rich area in a big city, until you get it, you will be working very hard. You will become focused on that goal and may not be fully happy in your daily life until the house is manifested. Most importantly, you will miss many opportunities to be in the present, live your life in flow and let your perfect house show up when it is time.

If you want a beautiful house in the future, start by making your present living situation beautiful. "Be your house" wherever that is. Bring lots of light energy into your life. That will create happiness, health and love and shape your future house with strong pillars.

It is the same thing with finding a loving partner. Don't try to manifest that person. Rather, love yourself, become love, trust and surrender. That is a better way to attract love. Stay in the present and have trust that the flow of life will lead you to your love partner.

If you want abundance, be abundance. When you think you are abundant, energetically you attract abundance. There is no need to try to manifest abundance in the future. If you feel that you are not good enough now, see yourself as more than enough now rather than trying to manifest being enough in the future. There will never be a future as we live in the present.

Let go of all conditioning that you are not good enough. To think you are not enough is only a perception of your past conditioning.

Light energy is everywhere and can recharge your machine in a day, the day you decide to be enough.

Take the decision to be in the present and be you. Be your house. Shine love all around. Be and feel abundant and you will start feeling more than enough.

Think about all the people trying to manifest their desires before they die. In their pursuit, they do not fully live here and now. They probably behave a certain way that is in-line with their conditioning-manifestation loop. They might succeed in some of their desires or what looks good to others but never live in the present WOW that a healthy machine will give them.

If you acknowledge that you are in the best machine ever and are grateful for it everyday, this will attract more than by trying to manifest anything in the future.

By being grateful, the laws of nature will be there for you and provide any information that you need for a WOW life.

Expressing gratitude everyday will automatically bring you to a state of being enough. It will only get better from this point onwards.

I am sure I am irritating lots of egos or the conditioning of people that are having trouble accepting this chapter or even the beginning of this book. But please, keep your programming in check. Be open and soon you will feel the power of your machine connecting with you because of the love you will be creating by caring for it.

This connection will put you on track for a beautiful journey.

THE ENERGY OF TIME

NERVOUS SYSTEM

TIME WAS CREATED BY THE MACHINE AS A TOOL TO COORDINATE WITH EVERYTHING. Everything is energy.

Your machine has tasks to do in life which use time and energy. That is the energy of time.

Should we, sitting inside our machine, be affected, controlled or under pressure of the energy of time? No. We should not. Let's see how.

Staying present in your machine is one way to stay healthy in light energy.

You can choose to help your machine by choosing to like what you are doing in the moment. Don't let your conditioning or manifestations, set earlier in your life, affect what you are doing now.

For example, you have to go to work tomorrow at 7 a.m. and you set your alarm for 6 a.m. That's for the machine to be on time for work but you have the capacity to stay in the present. If you start being controlled by time, you will be at work in your mind from the moment you set your alarm.

How can you change that? When you set your alarm at night, say thank you to your machine for the beautiful day you have had and set a beautiful intention for tomorrow. Wish it a good night and let it rest. Afterwards, you can see yourself wherever you want, like on a warm beach. Smell the breeze of the ocean, listen to the music of the waves and fall asleep. You can feel timeless and have restful sleep.

Now when you wake up and go to work, do your best in the moment, which will bring you to the next moment and the next without stressing over time. If you focus on time, you will use light energy on top of your machine already using energy.

Preserving your light energy will help you at work when you need it, for example, for making good decisions.

Intuition and synchronicity will guide you throughout your day, while you stay present and focused on your tasks.

Think about when you are with a person that you love. Time seems to stop and suddenly you realize this is what it feels like to live in the present and be on the frequency of love! You became timeless for a moment because you are not focused on time but rather in the present.

Aim to be in the present moment in everything you do and do it with love.

When you are on a love frequency, time dissolves.

THE ENERGY OF MONEY

MUSCULAR

MONEY IS A POWERFUL INVENTION BY THE MACHINE.

I was conditioned from a young age how important money is, what I am supposed to do with it and how much I should have. For most of my life, I let my happiness and self worth be valued by it.

As you saw in the energy chart, worrying about money is -500 energy units per day! Money has built systems of fairness and stability in this economic world but on the other hand, people have killed and started wars for it.

Try to bring yourself to where you don't have to worry about money on a daily basis. It's not about becoming rich or having a very well paid job. It's about being happy and loving what you do, and at the same time caring for your machine with the money necessary. People with lots of money can still worry if they don't deal properly with the energy of money. This is a major thing to understand.

Don't lose your energy over money. You need to detach from any negative programming about money and slowly find a balance between the energy of money and light energy, which will bring you peace of mind.

I have been dealing with the energy of money most of my life. It's been difficult to deal with this powerful energy. It affected me mentally, and also many of my romantic relationships, friendships and family dynamics. Many times I chose money instead of happiness thinking happiness will come with money.

What's my relationship with the energy of money now?
I understand it better. Only recently have I started to be good with it and not let it affect my decisions or how I'm feeling about situations. Now I know how much I need and how not to get stressed over it.

Should you try to manifest money? No! You may be thinking, "What?" No money manifestation for the future?

Stay focused on the present and create light energy from the seven principles. Believe in the power of the healthy machine and slowly that will make the energy of money part of you, not a desire.

That's the way I manage my energy about money now and I always have more than my machine needs to keep going while keeping my stress level in balance.

Money doesn't bring you happiness. Light energy does.

THE ENERGY OF INTENTIONS

INTEGUMENTARY

MY INTENTION WAS TO KEEP THIS CHAPTER FOR LAST BUT MY INTUITION TOLD ME DIFFERENTLY.

I experienced a big shift when I decided to detach from everything that people wanted me to be.

I am now here to help all machines have the chance to reach their optimal functionality as soon as possible, no matter what conditioning they may have or situation they are in. I know too well that in life we do what we think is right for ourselves from our conditioning and we end up in a situation that seems impossible to get out of. Sometimes it's the only way we know.

At the age of 44, it was clear that I was not happy in my life creation. I then made an intention to be happy.

Over the years, I had many signs from the universe to take a different direction in my life and I finally did. I put my restaurant and house up for sale without thinking of the future. I had no clue what was waiting for me and which direction to go but I was willing to take the risk of listening to my intuition regardless of what my conditioning and previous manifestations were telling me.

After 20 years of being successful at manifesting my desired life, it was hard to stay aligned with my new decision to do something new that would not be attached to conditioning, success or money.

It felt similar to quitting an addiction but at the same time, I was determined to try to feel good and to trust my capacity to create lasting happiness. That became my intention.

After selling my home and business, I travelled for six months, looked at the idea of operating an adventure business and, while living on Saltspring Island in B.C., Canada, took an online course on life coaching.

Next, I found myself volunteering and living in my tiny camping trailer on a yoga farm on the island.

However, I was still attached to the idea of who I used to be and to what I thought I should be doing now at my age.

I felt that I was losing my use of time. I didn't know how to detach myself from time at that moment.

Yet, within myself I felt good for the first time in a long time. I felt free. Moments of bliss would bubble up and all I wanted was more of it. Big changes were occurring from things that I was not aware of.

Some of the changes were the new fuel for my machine, daily meditation and yoga at the farm. I was in a community living mostly outside in nature, breathing fresh air and surrounded by water. All the principles of creating light energy came to me somehow, only by making an intention a year earlier of wanting to be happy.

I am writing this book to help you to bypass some steps.

Your machine is from Mother Nature and was connected to it at birth. Today, I'm asking you to make an intention to fully re-connect your machine to Nature. Also, by making this intention, the Consciousness-of-All will start working for you.

Start living your life by using the seven principles for more light energy and see how good your machine will feel. You might not have known the power of your machine until now.

When your machine starts to be WOW, there will be no need to worry, no need to plan the rest of your life and no need to check with past conditioning to see if each decision is good or not.

Be happy now with creating light energy everyday, connect with Nature and let the rest unfold by itself.

Everyone will have a different outcome, path and speed of experiencing everything but understand that through your intention

Mother Earth has heard you, will welcome you back and will accept you no matter where you are coming from.

When you fully re-connect your machine to Mother Nature, your life will change like it did for me.

ENERGY VOICES & DECISIONS

CARDIOVASCULAR

ARE YOU IN CHARGE OF YOUR DECISIONS? Why is it that some days you feel that you can't make a decision or are making bad ones? What voices inside you are telling you what to do? Is it possible that your environment is influencing your decisions?

Let's see …

Let's say that in your machine there are 100 energy voices to vote for a decision.

Some of those energy voices might have been contaminated over the years from conditioning or bad choices of fuel, friends, environment, etc.

The other ones are what I call transitioning voices. They are also affected by everything that you are in contact with and that enters your machine daily. The food you are eating, the water you're drinking, the air you are breathing, your relationships, contacts with nature, your work and the place you live will all affect your decisions.

If a machine is polluted with junk food, what type of decision do you think it will make?

If you change your diet to a plant-based one, you will think more clearly. I remember the first time that I ate a raw, plant-based diet for six days, 15 years ago, when a girlfriend challenged me. WOW. My mind became clearer and sharper after only a couple of days.

I even beat my brother, a chess champion, at chess for the first time in my life. I had no idea what was happening at the time. Looking back, I felt like something beyond myself was making the decisions for every move I made in the game.

Words and acts of love coming your way will influence your energy voices. Think about someone saying that they love you. You instantly become a better person within. This will change the way you talk and act until those energy voices influence you. Isn't that amazing! We are from the energy of love. It's easy to align with love and transmit it to others. Be open to love, become love and give love.

Love is one of my principal Sources. My belief is in humans who thrive, talk and act with love.

If you believe in God, Buddha or good aliens, that's okay too. No matter if your Source is different, if your energy or intentions are on the frequency of love, that's what is important.
The frequency of love is all around you. It travels through you to others. You have choices on how to receive it, keep it inside or keep it going.

Let's take a real example that is close to me. My mom was diagnosed with bone marrow cancer six years ago. For ten years before this, she was already eating very healthily, drank freshly made juice everyday, walked for one to two hours a day in nature, biked and cross-country skied. She meditated and did some yoga.

When the doctor told her the bad news, she checked within for a decision about what to do to keep living a long life.

My belief is that she had a larger number of good voices inside her which probably told her that there were other options for her, better options than what the doctor told her based on statistics. She listened to her voices and she's in amazing health today at the age of 75 and just got a bicycle for her birthday.

That story says that you have to keep a higher level of good voices inside at all times. You never know when a decision for your life will come your way. The voices voting are for everyday decisions but also for the big ones:

- » Getting married
- » Buying a house
- » What to study
- » Business partners
- » Children
- » Career
- » Bad news
- » Money

Over the years, you might have discovered that you made some bad decisions and you are now asking yourself, "What happened?" Your energy voices may have made the decisions for you.

Healthy voices are from our Source, nature and love in the form of words.

The words you use affect the energy that surrounds you. Use loving words to get on a love frequency.

Words will determine your reality and affect the flow of your life. Always use beautiful words.

This explains why my writing is sometimes short and not specific enough for some. I have kept it very positive and have eliminated all unnecessary negative words that can affect the energy of this book and simultaneously your energy.

Don't forget that you are somehow dependent on your inner voices for making instant decisions and you know now that some of those voices could be misleading you in life.

I have found somehow, with my new constant higher light energy, that it's easy to use beautiful words that match my new frequency of surrender, love and trust. That is the opposite of the control, hate and fear frequencies that many machines are on.

Be aware of the language you are using. Always use beautiful words. It will help balance your frequency for better decisions.

THE MACHINE VS. THE HUMAN

ENDOCRINE

SINCE THE BEGINNING OF THE BOOK, I DESCRIBED OUR HUMAN BODY AS A MACHINE. Halfway through writing the book, I had some people read the chapters that I had written and they questioned my use of the word machine. I put a lot of thought around this and tried to find other words that had the meaning of what I was envisioning. But I kept the "machine".

Most humans became something like a machine thousands of years ago due to many generations of conditioning.

They lost connection with their pristine powers and how to use them. They became passengers in their machine.

Are you the driver or the passenger of your machine?

When you decide to make the intention for a healthy life and take back control of your machine, from that moment you become the driver in your human body. You are not a machine anymore that was programmed and on cruise control with you sitting in the back watching your life unfold like a movie. Now you are the driver, driving your human body where the light energy is abundant and where the WOW is.

Take a look at what the differences are between the machine and human body.

- When a Machine becomes a Human Body
- The passenger becomes the driver
- The past and future become the present
- Conditioning becomes part of consciousness
- Manifestations becomes the flow of life
- Dark energy becomes light energy
- Expectations become intentions
- Anxiety becomes trust
- Wondering becomes intuition
- You become the miracle

When your machine transitions back to a human body, when you push your barriers or limitations of what you think you are supposed to be and do, when you and your body are in sync and full of vibrant light energy, you will become the miracle that you were designed to be from the beginning.

That is actually what Og Mandino's message is in his famous book, *The Greatest Miracle in the World*, one of the first books I read.

You are the miracle.

THE PUZZLE OF LIFE

SKELETAL

LET'S IMAGINE YOU HAVE TO MAKE A 1,000-PIECE PUZZLE WHILE ALIVE ON EARTH. The pieces will gradually come throughout your life.

Everyone has a unique puzzle. Some have a simple one and others have one that is more complex.

During life, you will meet people who have a piece for you to build your puzzle. If you are not receptive to receiving it, people will keep showing up with similar pieces until you understand the message.

This is the importance of a healthy body; your body will be open to receive pieces. Synchronicities will increase and life will flow.

Also, pieces will transit through you to give to others since energy flows between everyone.

The more you turn towards others, the more you will also learn about yourself.

If your programming taught you to build your puzzle from the bottom to the top, there is a good chance you'll get frustrated and stuck waiting for a piece for no reason.

Let go and everything will align in the flow of life.

It is the same if you swim against the current in a river, eventually you will get tired, let go and go right back to where you started. It is easier to swim with the current, with the flow of life.

There are different flows available to you.

Your flow will depend on your light energy. If you have low light energy, your flow will reflect that.

When you have a healthier body, your light energy increases and this simultaneously puts you in a better flow of life.

If you don't like the image of your puzzle, probably because it was built from your conditioning or manifestation, put it back in the box and start another one. That's life!

You have as many attempts as you want to change your puzzle. Don't try to manifest what you think you need or want. Instead, let the puzzle form itself, like everything in Nature does. Become light energy. Stay open. Your puzzle will form in front of you.

LOVE ENERGY

REPRODUCTIVE

WHEN TWO LOVE ENERGIES MEET

While I was writing this book, I flew from Vancouver to Montreal to visit my family. The night before my flight, I asked myself: "What is it about love that creates the ultimate energy?"

While on the plane next day, I kept focusing on the question and wrote the following. Love energy is when two people connect in the present from their free will and are ready to stay there for the love of each other.

Love energy is the greatest energy that you can experience and become. Even after you die, that energy will survive.

Remember, everything happens in the present. People that live in the past or the future will have difficulty accessing the love energy.

That is not to say that they can't share their past or plans for the future, as long as they realize that love energy is in the present.

Let's go back to my girlfriend story that I mentioned earlier in the book. Writing parts of this book made me realize what happened and how I discovered love energy and succeeded in using it beyond my relationship.

Four years before meeting her I started, without knowing it, practicing all the principles in this book. By doing so, I increased my level of light energy, probably to a peak of 500 a day. This was the first time in my life that I was able to care for my machine for more than a short period of time and create lasting happiness for myself.

I met her at that time in my life where I was at a high level of light energy. I fell for her pretty fast and definitely thought she was "the one".

For almost six months, we were simply friends because she was still involved in a relationship. When she left her relationship, we were able to start seeing each other for more than a coffee and started to know each other better. From a light energy of 500 a day on average, I was now experiencing peaks of 1,000. One thousand is very powerful. I was feeling invincible. I thought I was the luckiest guy in the world, my energy felt electric and I started loving and trusting life like never before. I had several peaks of the love energy with her when she was able to stay in that energy in the present. I am so grateful for those moments.

I had met other women previously in my life but I never started those relationships at the level of light energy I did in this relationship.

It's for that reason that I experienced that level of energy of 1,000 and all the powers that came with it.

However, she was not able to stay in the present in our relationship and give it more time to succeed.

Many short breakups happened. I felt that she was pushing me away because of her conditioning and then she was pulling me back by listening to her heart. This happened until she said that she needed to do what she felt was right for her. Her programming about what defines "the one" was different than what she saw in me.

From that breakup, I dropped to a low level of light energy, probably around zero. I wondered after a couple of weeks if it was possible to reach the level I had with her but without being with her. The answer that came to me was "Let's try". My idea was to keep loving thoughts for her, even if everything in me wanted to blame her. As hard as that seems, I challenged myself to go that route. I will say that I succeeded at reaching the highest peak of love energy ever in my life without a partner.

When you are able to experience and stay at that level, your pristine human powers start working for you in a way that is now noticeable.

You become love energy.

Love is the most powerful energy; humans were created from love, connected to everything in Nature and beyond.

However, most of us slowly detached from Mother Nature. We started thinking we should be better because we thought we were not good enough, we didn't like ourselves or the way we had been created.

We started altering and creating new foods, started manifesting prosperity for ourselves, created our own gods, started stealing from Mother Nature, and started wars against others.

You started life from love and have to get back to that frequency. It is ideal for you to vibrate with love in everything you do.

Love yourself by being grateful, by caring for your human body and by giving love to others. Give love with beautiful words and all your actions.

By doing so, you will be creating a love vibration within yourself and this will expand to everything through your love frequency!

You will be back to vibrating love and one day it will be your way out of this dimension. Love is the secret.

YOUR ENERGY IS READY

RESPIRATORY

NOW THAT YOU HAVE MADE YOUR INTENTION, IT'S TIME TO GET SERIOUS.

I'm inviting you to follow the principles in this book, yes even the fuel, for one to three weeks. I know many readers may be triggered by my suggested fuel for their machine. However, you can benefit from eating that way. Your machine will start glowing and you will begin to think differently. Life will shift dramatically from this simple commitment. You will rise from any darkness.

You will face resistance from many people around you because of their programming but I highly recommend that you continue on this path for one to three weeks and re-evaluate your light energy. See for yourself how your machine is starting to feel and how you are transforming.

If you are pushing your body to the limit, for example with too much stress, it will tell you with pain. It is the way it is designed. Understanding this is the beginning of understanding love, love for yourself. If you go too long without listening to your body's signs, Nature might have to redirect you.

When you reach a high level of love energy, you become love energy. Your desires become part of everything and everything knows it before you do.

You will now desire nothing because you will be everything. Everything is within you. You will be one with everything, connected to Nature and the Consciousness-of-All.

You are part of Nature and are connected to the elements. You are living in the now. Get back to the elements and reconnect to Mother Nature and the Flow. That is the beginning of your new energy.

If you don't water a plant or if you keep it in the dark, it will deteriorate. You only need to put it back in its element where it belongs among its friends and in a healthy environment for it to thrive.

Instead of feeling you are not good enough, focus on the positive, be grateful for who you are, raise your light energy and recognize that you are a miracle, you are WOW.

You were WOW at the beginning of your life. At any moment you can decide to start again with love and return to the state of WOW.

When it comes to WOW energy, you know it! WOW energy feels like a vibration that bounces in your human body like excited electrons.

Rather than living life from programming, imagine living it from the WOW energy state instead. WOW is only in the present.

Practice slowing down and taking your time to feel WOW. Stay in the flow of life, surrendering with love and trust, and all the WOW moments, people, experiences, jobs and partners will naturally synchronize for you.

If you want to make sure that a feeling of WOW is not just temporary, sleep on it and see if you wake up with the same WOW vibration the next day. If you do, it's a yes. It may take time for you to feel long lasting and meaningful WOW.

If you are running on dark energy, you can mistake something as WOW, yet it is not. This mistake can keep you in the loop of dark energy longer. This is why it's so important to get into light energy each day as soon as possible for the energy voices to help you with WOW decisions.

If you are in the middle of transitioning from the dark to the light, from programming to WOW, from old habits to new principles, here is a warning: transitions can be hard and scary. Any attempt to get out of programming or comfort zones will be this way. It can be hard to feel the WOW during that period.

WOW is an innate truth. It is a feeling within you. Lots of light energy is waiting for you.

FROM LOVE TO YOU

FROM THE INTENTION TO BE HAPPY, OVER THE LAST FIVE YEARS I INTUITIVELY FOLLOWED PRINCIPLES THAT BECAME PART OF ME.

I started understanding more of my surrounding energies and how those affected me daily. I started asking questions of my Source and received answers.

I also realized that my life was better with no more conditioning, no more manifesting, no more stress over my use of time and no more worries about the energy of money. By doing so, I got on the love, surrender and trust frequency where everything started to be WOW for me.

I became this book, I became love and I became WOW. I started living my life in harmony and in the present.

You can do the same.

To this day, what I have written in this book keeps popping up in my head about how much of it is right, and since it is, how easy it could be for us to change little things in life that can affect so much for us and simultaneously for Mother Earth.

When I almost lost everything years ago and when my recent relationship ended, both times I understood somehow that in situations that hurt my energy, I had to let go, even if it meant the end of something that was feeling good.

I understood that I had to go back to my Source and focus on loving. I know now that there is always a new experience or something even better waiting for me.

When you follow the principles in this book, you go from being a machine that was defined by your conditioning, surroundings and what you created for yourself, to a beautiful energy radiating into the world.

You will be everything you want because everything is part of your new energy.

You will become WOW with all your super powers within.

The best way I can explain this for now, because my understanding is still evolving, is that it is the feeling of being everything, wanting nothing and being in love. It is a constant WOW state within.

As it happens for me, everything around you will start flowing with you, sometimes even in front of you. Recently, people have said, "It seems so easy for you to manage your life now. How do you do it?" My answer is always that it is the WOW energy. When you become WOW, everything around you flows in the energy you are radiating.

Be grateful for the beautiful energy that you are, feel it and let it flow outward.

From the frequency of Love to You, may the WOW be with you.

CONCLUDING TALK ABOUT THE BOOK BY LAWRENCE AND MARTIN

Lawrence: Can you give me an analogy to better understand light energy?

Martin: Imagine you have a very powerful light bulb (1,000 Watts) inside you that corresponds to the maximum light energy that you can attain and that you want to keep it as bright as possible each day.

The brightness of your light bulb influences your flow in life, the frequency you are on and your ability to use your super powers.

Your happiness, even your life, depends on your light energy and you need to do everything possible to keep it as bright as you can.

Let's say someone in your life is taking so much of your light energy that you lose your bright light and your happiness. What should you do? It is in your power to be aware of it and decide to minimize or stop it.

It is the same with fuel. As in my light energy chart in the book, some food will deplete you and some will light you up. You decide how radiant you want to be.

Movement makes your light bulb brighter.

When you breathe deeply for a period of time, you can see light even when your eyes are closed.

One of the ways to get the most energy for your light bulb is the energy of love. That energy will automatically make you shine.

Being outside in nature, in the sun or even in the rain, provides light energy.

Always think of the inside of your body as a light bulb and keep it shining as brightly you can. That will show everyone where you are at and who you are. It will show the consciousness-of-all that you are receptive to the energy- and information-of-everything.

The brighter your light bulb, the easier it will be to see clearly and feel the WOW inside you and shine your light on the world around you.

Lawrence: You are saying in the book that there is another, different flow of life. What do you mean?

Martin: The energy level that you maintain will determine your flow. It will change the current of your life.

Everything is energy. It can range from highly positive to highly negative. Start by being aware of your energy. The everyday little changes that you do will change your flow in life.
When you become aware, you have access to free will and that gives you access to a different flow in life.

Lawrence: How do you know you're in the right flow?

Martin: When your light energy is at a good level, everything in your life flows easily and will help you discover your purpose in life.

Lawrence: You say in your book that if you breathe better, talk to the water you are going to drink and eat a plant-based diet, everything can change. Is it that simple?

Martin: All those things are about taking care of yourself on a daily basis. This raises your light energy, puts you in a positive flow and you eventually connect with everything. You have to surrender in that process, let go of the control from conditioning, let go of trying to manifest your future. Trust that process and do it with love, and yes, it will be that simple.

Lawrence: What's your recommendation for someone to start?

Martin: Love yourself by doing the right things, such as what I cover in the book.

Look for love around you, in people, at work and in all situations. You will rise from any darkness by following acts of love. Start with love, look for it and become love.

Lawrence: In your chapter about energy voices and decisions, you say that the decisions we make in life are influenced by the food we eat. How did you come up with that idea?

Martin: I just became aware of the influence of my change of diet and the new person I became. From that I searched for understanding.

I started looking at the people I know, what they eat and who they are in life.

I also thought of people that were struggling with addiction or living on the street. What food did they eat while growing up and what do they eat now? Does that affect their current situation?

I looked at dictators and people who started wars, compared to those who wanted peace? I found it fascinating to think that there could be a correlation with the food they ate. That's where my idea came from.

Lawrence: With all your new knowledge and light energy, what is next for you?

Martin: One thing that creating this book helped me discover is that mostly everything that is good comes from love. My intention is to try to use as much unconditional love in my life as possible. Less judgement of others and myself and no more hate, dislikes or negative words directed at anyone or anything. This should allow me to create a new reality for myself. It will also send a message to others and to this beautiful consciousness that connects all creation. I know what I'm saying here is not going to be an easy task but that is my intention. I really believe that good can happen as a result of unconditional love.

Lawrence: This book took two years to write and you put an enormous amount of thought into creating it. What a wonderful gift you have created for others to experience.

Martin: Thanks Lawrence. Thanks also for all the beautiful time we spent together on this book. This amazing friendship we have, even considering our different backgrounds, life experiences and age, we managed to bring this book to publication and we are still hanging out for coffee or walks. Thanks for your trust, patience, support and mostly friendship.

WOW. Life is beautiful.